AN ESTUARY Food Chain

A WHO-EATS-WHAT
Adventure in
North America

Rebecca Hogue Wojahn Donald Wojahn

Lerner Publications Company
Minneapolis

For Eli and Cal. We hope this answers some of your questions.

There are many links in the chain that created this series. Thanks to Susan Rose, Carol Hinz, Danielle Carnito, Sarah Olmanson, Paul Rodeen, the staff of the L. E. Phillips Memorial Public Library, and finally, Katherine Hogue

Lerner Publications Company
A division of Lerner Publishing Group, Inc.
241 First Avenue North
Minneapolis, MN 55401 U.S.A.

Website address: www.lernerbooks.com

Library of Congress Cataloging-in-Publication Data

Wojahn, Rebecca Hogue.
   An estuary food chain : a who–eats–what adventure in North America / by Rebecca Hogue Wojahn and Donald Wojahn.
     p.   cm. — (Follow that food chain)
   Includes bibliographical references and index.
   ISBN 978-0-8225-7616-7 (lib., bdg. : alk. paper)
   1. Estuarine ecology—North America—Juvenile literature. 2. Food chains (Ecology)—North America—Juvenile literature. I. Wojahn, Donald. II. Title.
QH541.5.E8W62 2010
577.7'8616—dc22   2009007242

Manufactured in the United States of America
1 2 3 4 5 6 – BP – 15 14 13 12 11 10

Contents

Introduction
WELCOME TO THE ESTUARY

The closer the Mississippi River gets to the Gulf of Mexico, the spongier the ground is. Moss-draped trees rise from the bayous and swamps along the river. Green duckweed blankets ponds, covering the still water underneath. In some places, sandy shorelines peek through, but other places are sticky with mud and tangled with plants. Sea grasses ripple in the tides. For the most part, it's hard to tell what's land and what's water. It's hard to tell exactly where the river ends and the gulf begins.

The soggy land between a river and a sea is called an estuary. The 4-million-acre (1.6-million-hectare) estuary at the Mississippi Delta is the largest in North America. It's also disappearing before our eyes. People reroute water and fill swamps so houses don't flood. They build dams and locks, and those keep the river from bringing new soil to the area. **Native** plants and trees can't grow in the changing soil. And without the roots of the plants and trees to hold the soil in place, the gulf eats away at the land. Every forty-five minutes, 1 acre (0.4 hectares) of the marshy barrier between land and sea is lost to the sea.

Millions of plants and animals call the estuary home. Some animals just visit from other habitats. Birds from South America flock in to raise their young in a safe place. Ocean fish lay their eggs in the shallows where bigger fish can't eat them. When these young animals get big and strong enough, they leave. But others live their whole lives here, such as the alligator snapping turtle hiding under the duckweed, the crayfish scuttling in the shallows, and the biting midges hatching in the sand. Come meet just a few of these **species** in this book.

Estuary

N

Mississippi River

UNITED STATES

Louisiana

Mississippi

Gulf of Mexico

Choose a
TERTIARY CONSUMER

All the living things in the estuary are necessary for its health and survival. From the American alligator lurking just under the water to the nematode scuttling through the dead leaves, all living things are connected. Some animals feed on other animals. Other animals eat plants. Plants collect energy from the sun and **nutrients** from the soil. This is called a **food chain**. Energy is transferred from one member of the chain to another. In every **habitat**, food chains are linked together to become a **food web**.

In a food web, the strongest **predators** are called **tertiary consumers**. They hunt other animals for food and have few natural enemies. Some of the animals they eat are called **secondary consumers**. Secondary consumers are also predators. They hunt plant-eating animals. Plant-eating animals are **primary consumers**.

Plants are **producers**. Using energy from the sun and nutrients from the soil, they produce their own food. They provide nutrients to the animals that eat them.

Decomposers are animals or **bacteria** that break down dead plants and animals. Decomposers return nutrients from the dead plants and animals to the soil.

The plants and animals in a food web depend on one another. Sometimes there's a break in a chain, such as one animal species dying out. This loss ripples through the rest of the habitat.

Begin your journey through the estuary food web by choosing a large **carnivore**, or meat eater. These tertiary consumers are at the top of the food chain. That means that as healthy adults, they don't have any enemies in the estuary.

When it's time for the tertiary consumer to eat, choose its meal and flip to that page. As you go through the book, don't be surprised if you backtrack and end up where you never expected to be. That's how food webs work—they're complicated. And watch out for those dead ends! That's when a species is **endangered** or **extinct** and there aren't enough animals alive to feed another species. When you hit a dead end, go back to page 7 and start over with another tertiary consumer.

The main role a plant or animal plays in the estuary food web is identified by a color-coded shape. Here is the key to that code:

TERTIARY CONSUMER

PRODUCER

SECONDARY CONSUMER

PRIMARY CONSUMER

DECOMPOSER

To choose . . .

. . . an American alligator, TURN TO PAGE 8.

. . . a bobcat, TURN TO PAGE 19.

. . . a spotted gar, TURN TO PAGE 32.

. . . an alligator snapping turtle, TURN TO PAGE 47.

. . . a barred owl, TURN TO PAGE 53.

To learn more about an estuary food web, GO TO PAGE 34.

AMERICAN ALLIGATOR *(Alligator mississippiensis)*

The American alligator glides through the swampy water. Only her eyes and nose peek above the surface. Her 8-foot-long (2.4 m) body is hidden from sight. Behind her, the green duckweed swirls as her tail swings back and forth. Her tail silently propels her through the water. Near the shore, the alligator hauls herself out of the swampy water. Her

An alligator pops its head through the duckweed.

stubby legs are awkward on land. But she's right where she needs to be. For the last two months, she hasn't strayed far from this mound—3 feet (1 m) high, 6 feet (2 m) wide—of mud and weeds on the shore. The sun has baked it, and it's hard and crusty.

She tramps around the mound to a mud puddle and slides on her belly right into it. Her arrival scatters a heron, a nutria, and a couple of ducks. This is her hole, her home. She dug it out last spring, scraping the mud aside with her hind legs and tail, until the hole filled with water. Alligator holes like hers become miniature habitats within the estuary for all kinds of animals.

Almost Gone

Did you know alligators have been on this planet for 150 million years? Their ancestors swam with dinosaurs. Yet in recent years, alligators came very close to dying out. People hunted them and used their skins for purses and shoes. By the 1960s, alligators were on the verge of extinction. Luckily, people changed their minds about alligators and laws were passed to protect them. Alligators are again thriving in the swamps of southern North America.

9

As the alligator lounges in her hole, small fish swim around her. She doesn't bother with them. She ate earlier that day. For now they're safe. Suddenly, a tiny cry makes her lift her head. There it is again. A squeak. A chirp. The sounds are coming from the mound!

The alligator rushes to the mound. The cries come from deep inside. They are growing louder. With her front legs and her mouth, the alligator starts tearing into the mud of the mound. She uses her sharp claws and teeth to pull it apart. Finally, she uncovers forty eggs—her eggs—buried deep inside. The eggs chirp and squeak. Some are already cracking open.

One by one, alligator hatchlings break out of their shells. As they hatch, the mother alligator scoops them up in her mouth. Her tongue curls gently around them. She takes a mouthful of hatchlings to the water. In the water, she opens her mouth a crack and swishes her head back and forth. The hatchlings swim out of her mouth.

Once they are free, she turns back for another batch. When all the hatchlings are paddling in the water, the mother joins them. The hatchlings look like miniature versions of an adult alligator. But they are far from being independent. They'll need her protection for almost two years before they are ready to navigate the estuary on their own.

Last night for dinner, the American alligator chomped . . .

. . . an anhinga fishing near shore. To see what another anhinga is up to, TURN TO PAGE 25.

. . . a cottonmouth crossing the swamp. To see what another cottonmouth is up to, TURN TO PAGE 42.

. . . a spotted gar basking on the water's surface. To see what another spotted gar is up to, TURN TO PAGE 32.

. . . a whooping crane snacking on minnows. To see what another whooping crane is up to, TURN TO PAGE 46.

. . . a nutria swimming through the swamp. To see what another nutria is up to, TURN TO PAGE 35.

. . . a swamp rabbit grazing on water plants. To see what another swamp rabbit is up to, TURN TO PAGE 51.

. . . a northern raccoon washing his food in the water. To see what another northern raccoon is up to, TURN TO PAGE 58.

. . . a Virginia opossum getting a quick drink of water. To see what another Virginia opossum is up to, TURN TO PAGE 37.

CHANNEL CATFISH *(Ictalurus punctatus)*

The estuary is dark, but under the water's surface, the channel catfish is alert and watchful. He swims back and forth in front of a sunken log. When another fish approaches, the 3-foot-long (1-meter) catfish charges at it with his mouth open. The other fish scoots away, leaving the channel catfish to himself.

The catfish seems to be guarding something. Under the log, in a shallow hole, there's a yellowish glob of jelly. The glob is a batch of the catfish's eggs. Earlier, he and his mate fanned out the sand under the log so she could lay the eggs in a safe place. The eggs will hatch in a week or so. Even then the catfish will watch over his newborns, called fry.

Swimming back and forth in front of the nest, the catfish also searches for a meal for himself. Those "whiskers" around his face are called barbels. They help him to sense food. He skims the bottom, sucking in plants, crayfish, snails, dead fish, and whatever else he comes across. He's a **scavenger**. Further off, his mate does the same. He chased her off after she laid their eggs, but she hasn't left completely. She'll watch from afar.

Last night for dinner, the channel catfish gulped . . .

. . . a crayfish hiding beneath the layer of dead leaves underwater. To see what another crayfish is doing, TURN TO PAGE 30.

. . . a nematode that drifted out too far into the water. To see what another nematode is up to, TURN TO PAGE 16.

. . . an injured sheepshead minnow. To see what another sheepshead minnow is up to, TURN TO PAGE 44.

. . . a lesser siren swimming through the water. To see what another lesser siren is up to, TURN TO PAGE 22.

. . . bits of dead duckweed at the bottom of the water. To see what duckweed and other water plants are like, TURN TO PAGE 27.

. . . biting midge larva squiggling in the water. To see what biting midges are up to, TURN TO PAGE 56.

WOOD DUCK

(Aix sponsa)

The fluffy wood duckling teeters on the branch 60 feet (18 meters) above the water. Already, all eleven of her siblings have taken the plunge. Her mother calls for her from the water below. *Oooo-eek! Oooo-eek!*

The wood duckling wobbles in the breeze. The warm feather and wood-chip-filled nest is behind her. She hatched there just twenty-four hours ago. But her mother is insistent. *Oooo-eek!*

The duckling steps out into the air. Her fluffy wings aren't ready for flying yet. She spins and tumbles through the air. Down, down, down, then—splash! She hits the water.

The duckling bobs up. Suddenly her siblings surround her. Her mother is just ahead. The wood duckling tries out her webbed feet in the water. She paddles to her mother. On the way, she pecks at the water bugs that are skating on the surface. The duckling is learning fast. With another call, her mother gathers all her ducklings. And the family swims off in search of more food.

Last night for dinner, the mother wood duck ate . . .

A female *(left)* and male wood duck

14

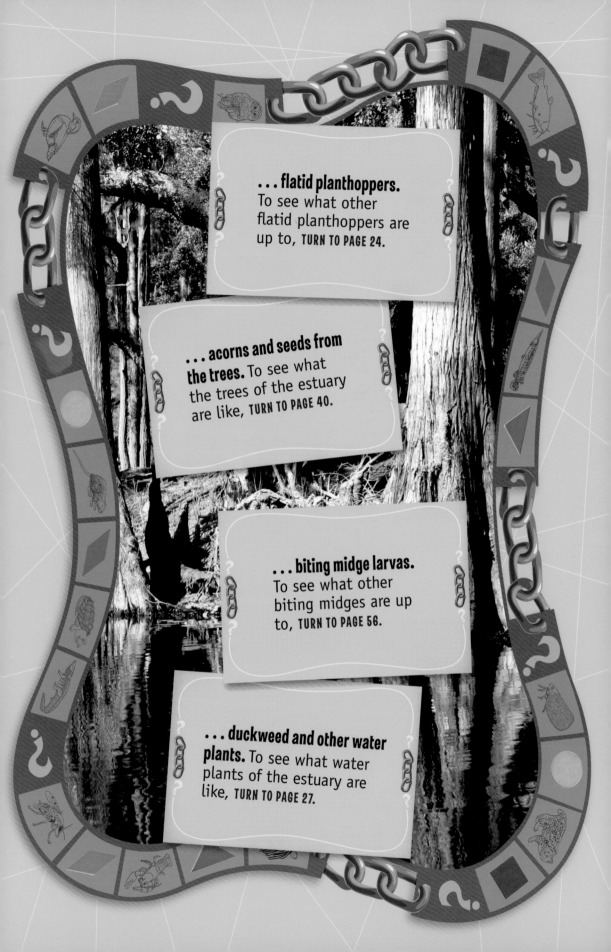

. . . flatid planthoppers. To see what other flatid planthoppers are up to, **TURN TO PAGE 24.**

. . . acorns and seeds from the trees. To see what the trees of the estuary are like, **TURN TO PAGE 40.**

. . . biting midge larvas. To see what other biting midges are up to, **TURN TO PAGE 56.**

. . . duckweed and other water plants. To see what water plants of the estuary are like, **TURN TO PAGE 27.**

NEMATODE (Nemata phylum)

Wriggling through the mud are thousands of nematodes. Some are microscopic, and some are visible as squiggling little worms. But others can grow to be several feet long! Many nematodes plow through the soil and dead plants on the floor of the estuary. They are sometimes described as a "tube within a tube." That's because as they move through the soil, they are eating it as well. The soil enters their mouths, passes through their digestive system, and exits their bodies. Along the way, the nematode digests the tiny bits of dead plants and animals.

Their presence in the soil helps break down the dead matter. That leaves the soil ready for new plants to grow.

Last night for dinner, the nematode digested tiny bits and pieces of...

Above: A group of nematodes feed on a dead slug.
Below: This microscopic nematode is known as a roundworm.

. . . a dead ivory-billed woodpecker. To see what another ivory-billed woodpecker is up to, TURN TO PAGE 18.

. . . a dead gray bat. To see what another gray bat is up to, TURN TO PAGE 50.

. . . a dead bobcat. To see what another bobcat is up to, TURN TO PAGE 19.

. . . dead biting midges. To see what other biting midges are up to, TURN TO PAGE 56.

. . . a dead anhinga. To see what another anhinga is up to, TURN TO PAGE 25.

Living Off Others

Not all nematodes get their food from dirt. Some are parasites. That means they live off other living creatures. Some dig their way into plants and live and eat there. Others get inside the bodies of animals. Even humans can have nematodes living inside them.

IVORY-BILLED WOODPECKER

(Campephilus principalis)

BAM-bam. BAM-bam. Years ago, the forests of the estuary echoed with the pounding of ivory-billed woodpeckers on hollow trees. But the southern forests were cut down for wood, and people moved in. That drove the ivory-billed woodpeckers out. For more than fifty years, no one could say for sure that they had seen one of the birds. So the species was declared extinct in 1994.

Then, in 2005, a group of scientists thought that they spied a male ivory-billed woodpecker in the woods in Arkansas. Maybe the bird wasn't extinct after all! Despite searching and offers of rewards, however, no further evidence has been found. That's why this is a *DEAD END*.

This ivory-billed woodpecker was stuffed many years ago.

The Lord God Bird

The ivory-billed woodpecker is also known as the Lord God Bird, or the Good God Bird. That's because when people would catch a glimpse of one, they almost always would exclaim, "Lord God!!!" or "Good God!!!" The bird—20 inches long (51 centimeters) with a wingspan of 30 inches (76 cm)—is the largest woodpecker. Its black-and-white body crowned with a bright red tuft of feathers, combined with its

BOBCAT *(Lynx rufus)*

The bobcat prowls along the trail bordering the edge of the water. Like most cats, her steps are silent. Her flecked coat blends in perfectly with the moonlit shadows of the night. She pauses, and her tufted ears swivel. Something's ahead!

She crouches, stealing forward through the brush, an inch at a time. An opossum nibbles on a late-night snack in the clearing ahead. The bobcat creeps around the opossum, waiting for just the right moment. Her chest is low against the ground. Her rear is raised, displaying her short "bobbed" tail.

Now! She springs forward, landing on the opossum with her front paws. One quick bite to the neck, and it's all over for the opossum.

The bobcat carries the dead opossum by the neck through the woods. She pokes her head into a hollow log. Two bobcat kittens mew at the smell of fresh meat. The mother bobcat pulls the opossum inside, and together the family dines on the mother's catch of the night.

Last night for dinner, the bobcat caught . . .

20

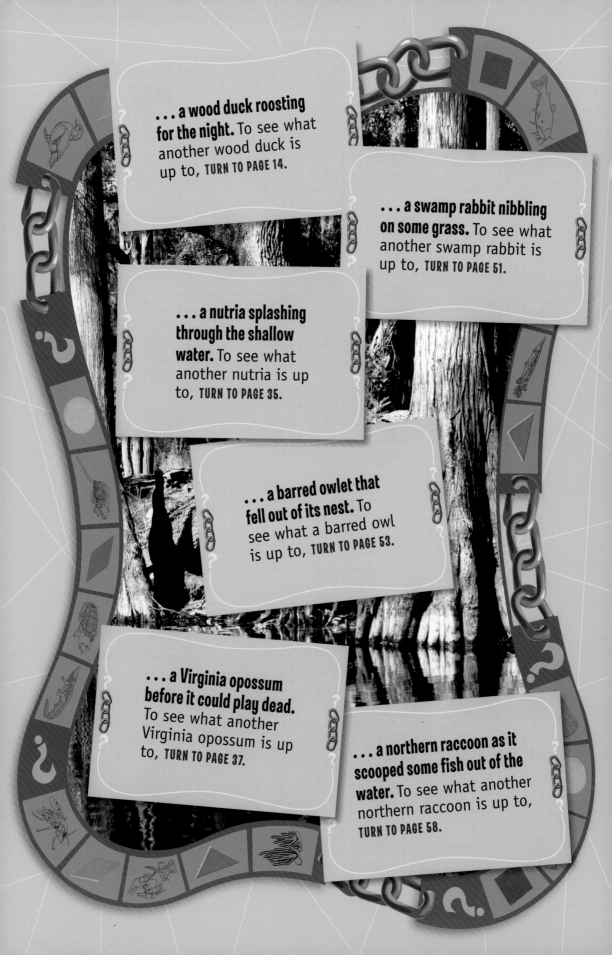

. . . a wood duck roosting for the night. To see what another wood duck is up to, TURN TO PAGE 14.

. . . a swamp rabbit nibbling on some grass. To see what another swamp rabbit is up to, TURN TO PAGE 51.

. . . a nutria splashing through the shallow water. To see what another nutria is up to, TURN TO PAGE 35.

. . . a barred owlet that fell out of its nest. To see what a barred owl is up to, TURN TO PAGE 53.

. . . a Virginia opossum before it could play dead. To see what another Virginia opossum is up to, TURN TO PAGE 37.

. . . a northern raccoon as it scooped some fish out of the water. To see what another northern raccoon is up to, TURN TO PAGE 58.

LESSER SIREN *(Siren intermedia)*

The sun rises higher in the sky, and the air grows hotter. The lesser siren wiggles its way deeper into the wet dead leaves at the edge of the water. She wants to stay wet—and hidden—during the day.

But just as she settles into a place, the long beak of a heron stabs through the mud. It just misses the lesser siren! With a push of her stubby front legs, the siren shoots through the shallow water to find a safer place to rest for the day. Her long body waves back and forth, propelling her through the water. She looks like a two-legged eel.

The siren finds a new hiding spot under a branch that's fallen into the water. Unlike many **amphibians**, she doesn't have to come up for air. She can breathe like a fish underwater. That's because she can get oxygen from the water through her gills. They're the feathery fringes at the sides of her head.

When night falls, the lesser siren will come out from her hiding place and hunt. *Last night for dinner, the lesser siren caught . . .*

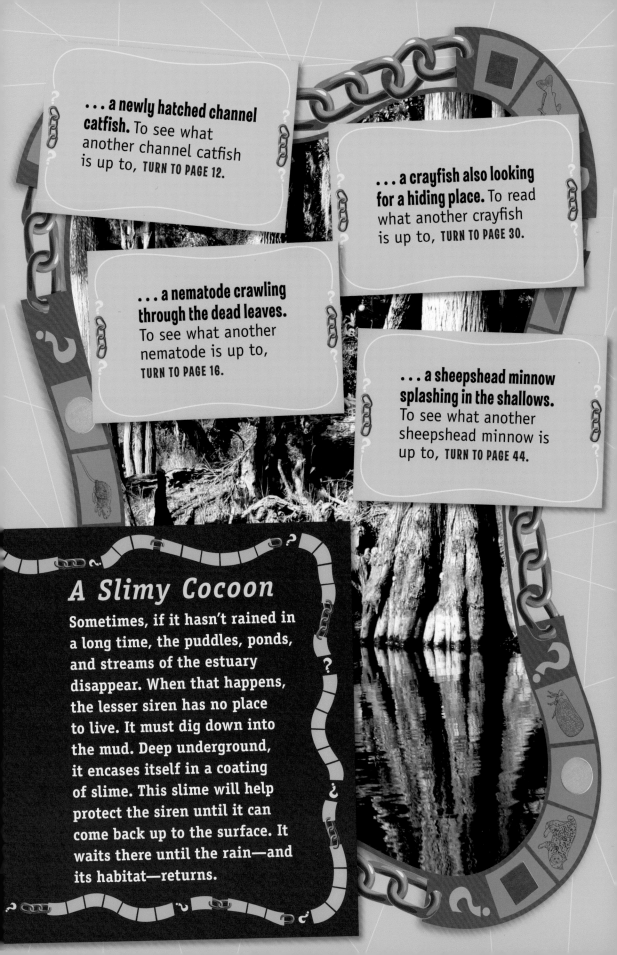

. . . **a newly hatched channel catfish.** To see what another channel catfish is up to, TURN TO PAGE 12.

. . . **a crayfish also looking for a hiding place.** To read what another crayfish is up to, TURN TO PAGE 30.

. . . **a nematode crawling through the dead leaves.** To see what another nematode is up to, TURN TO PAGE 16.

. . . **a sheepshead minnow splashing in the shallows.** To see what another sheepshead minnow is up to, TURN TO PAGE 44.

A Slimy Cocoon

Sometimes, if it hasn't rained in a long time, the puddles, ponds, and streams of the estuary disappear. When that happens, the lesser siren has no place to live. It must dig down into the mud. Deep underground, it encases itself in a coating of slime. This slime will help protect the siren until it can come back up to the surface. It waits there until the rain—and its habitat—returns.

FLATID PLANTHOPPER *(Flatidae spinola)*

Sproing! The wedge-shaped flatid planthopper springs off the leaf. It's hard to tell where she lands because she looks just like a leaf herself. She holds her light green wings behind her like a tent.

There she is—higher up on the trunk of the oak tree. The tiny bug slides her needlelike mouthparts into a green leaf. She sucks out a tiny bit of sap—not enough to harm the tree. As she drinks, she leaves a white, fluffy wax on the leaf.

If she's not disturbed, the planthopper will live her whole life on the tree. Later in the season, she'll slice small slits in the bark of the tree with her mouthparts. She'll lay her eggs in these slits. The eggs will hatch the next spring. The newly hatched planthoppers, called nymphs, will feed on the tree's tender new shoots. Then the nymphs will molt and become the size and shape of their mother.

Last night for dinner, the flatid planthopper sucked on . . .

24

. . . **the leaves of estuary trees.** To see what the trees of the estuary are like, **TURN TO PAGE 40.**

ANHINGA *(Anhinga anhinga)*

The anhinga paddles through the brackish water. Only her long neck and head stick out of the water. But she's not in danger of sinking. Her webbed feet push her through the water. As she nears the shore, the anhinga stabs her spiky beak at something underwater. She comes up with a fish speared on the end. She shakes her head to loosen the fish, but it's stuck. She swims to shore with the fish on her beak. Then she scrapes the fish off on a rock. She swallows it headfirst.

An anhinga dives to catch a fish.

The anhinga spreads her wings wide. Her feathers don't have the waterproof coating that the feathers of most waterbirds do, so she has to dry them. She can't fly until they dry a little more. While her wings dry, she has to be extra careful of predators lurking about.

25

After an hour of basking in the sun, the anhinga runs down the beach. She flaps her wings hard and takes off. A few more flaps, and she's cleared the treetops. Her wings stretch to a 4-foot (1.2-meter) wingspan. She soars high above the estuary for the rest of the day.

Last night for dinner, the anhinga speared . . .

This anhinga is drying itself in the sun.

. . . a channel catfish.
To see what another
channel catfish is
up to, TURN TO PAGE 12.

**. . . a young spotted
gar.** To see what a
spotted gar is up
to, TURN TO PAGE 32.

. . . a young cottonmouth.
To see what another
cottonmouth is up to,
TURN TO PAGE 42.

. . . a lesser siren. To
see what another
lesser siren is up
to, TURN TO PAGE 22.

WATER PLANTS OF THE ESTUARY

The green layer on the top of this pond is duckweed.

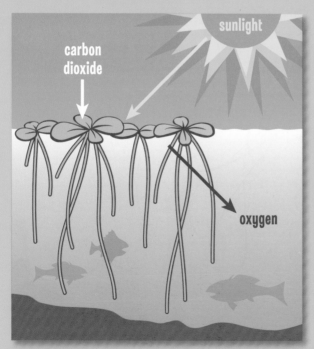

sunlight

carbon dioxide

oxygen

Plants make food and oxygen through photosynthesis. Plants draw in carbon dioxide (a gas found in air) and water. Then they use the energy from sunlight to turn the carbon dioxide and water into their food.

In the quiet backwaters of the estuary, still ponds are blanketed by tiny floating green leaves no wider than pencil erasers. That green layer is duckweed. It has no roots, just a dangling root hair. It grows in water with no current. As it spreads, it blocks the sun from the water. Other water plants can't grow, so they can't produce oxygen. In a duckweed-covered pond, there's not enough oxygen in the water.

eelgrass

pickerelweed

Sedges and cattails grow in the water where duckweed hasn't taken over. There's not a lot of air in the soil beneath the water, so some of these types of plants have hollow stems to bring air down to their roots. Eelgrass looks like tall grass growing entirely underwater. It flows and ripples with the tides and currents. Pickerelweed is rooted in the muddy bottom, but it has a heart-shaped leaf that floats on the surface.

In the salty water, cordgrass grows. Look closely and you'll see the salt crystals along the plants' stems. Those crystals form as the plants rid themselves of the excess salt.

The water plants feed the estuary's primary consumers. Plants need nutrients from the soil, which come from decomposing animals and plants. *Duckweed, sedges, cattails, eelgrass, pickerelweed, and cordgrass are growing from nutrients from . . .*

cordgrass

... a dead American alligator. To see what another American alligator is up to, TURN TO PAGE 8.

... a dead gray bat. To see what another gray bat is up to, TURN TO PAGE 50.

... a dead anhinga. To see what another anhinga is up to, TURN TO PAGE 25.

... a dead barred owl. To see what another barred owl is up to, TURN TO PAGE 53.

... a dead whooping crane. To see what another whooping crane is up to, TURN TO PAGE 46.

... a dead northern raccoon. To see what another northern raccoon is up to, TURN TO PAGE 58.

... a dead alligator snapping turtle. To see what another alligator snapping turtle is up to, TURN TO PAGE 47.

CRAYFISHES
(Astacidae family)

The 4-inch-long (10-centimeter) crayfish scoots along the muddy bottom of the bay with his four pairs of legs. He uses his two sets of antennas to follow the edge of a sunken log under the water.

The log rolls a little. Something's landed on it. A shadow falls across the water. The log has moved and uncovered the crayfish's hiding place. Suddenly, a beak stabs down through the water. The heron that landed on the log is hunting for its meal.

The crayfish uncurls his tail quickly. It shoots him backward, farther under the log and away from the heron. The quick movement stirs up the mud. The heron doesn't get a second chance to find the crayfish.

Deep in the shadows under the log, the crayfish continues its crawling search for food. He won't come out into the open until night falls. Meanwhile, a worm wiggles in front of him. The crayfish shoots forward. Snap! He catches the worm in his right claw. He snips and shreds the worm into bits. Then he brings the bits to his mouth to eat.

Last night for dinner, the crayfish ate . . .

Growing Pains

Crayfish can live for two to three years. During that time, as a crayfish grows, it sheds its shell. When an old shell splits, the crayfish crawls out of it. It takes several days for a new shell to harden, so the crayfish is in extra danger during that time. It has to stay hidden deep in the shadows and under the mud.

. . . a young channel catfish, called a fry. To see what a channel catfish is up to, TURN TO PAGE 12.

. . . a spotted gar fry. To see what a spotted gar is up to, TURN TO PAGE 32.

. . . a nematode wriggling in the mud. To see what another nematode is up to, TURN TO PAGE 16.

. . . a sheepshead minnow. To see what another sheepshead minnow is up to, TURN TO PAGE 44.

. . . a lesser siren swimming through the water. To see what another lesser siren is up to, TURN TO PAGE 22.

SPOTTED GAR *(Lepisosteus oculatus)*

The 3-foot-long (1-meter) spotted gar floats near the surface of the water. He basks in the sun-warmed water. The water is murky and still in this part of the estuary. But the gar is comfortable. Every so often, he sticks his long, thin snout out of the water and takes a breath of air. Most fish need clear water with lots of oxygen in it to breathe, but not the gar. He has a special swim bladder inside him. This swim bladder holds oxygen for him when he can't get enough from the water around him. When the oxygen in the water is low, he just gulps the oxygen-rich air.

The gar hasn't moved in over an hour. But as the sun starts to go down, he waves his long tail and glides slowly through the water. A quick silver flash in the murky water catches his eye. A minnow! With a quick flick of his tail, the gar zips around. His long, skinny shape slices through the water. Before the minnow can dodge, the gar's narrow mouth full of needle-sharp teeth snap down on it. The gar swallows the minnow headfirst. Then he heads toward deeper water, looking for something a little bigger to finish off his meal.

Last night for dinner, the spotted gar ate . . .

. . . a small channel catfish. To see what another channel catfish is up to, TURN TO PAGE 12.

. . . a crayfish. To see what another crayfish is up to, TURN TO PAGE 30.

. . . a wood duckling. To see what other wood ducks are up to, TURN TO PAGE 14.

. . . a lesser siren. To see what another lesser siren is up to, TURN TO PAGE 22.

. . . several sheepshead minnows. To see what other sheepshead minnows are up to, TURN TO PAGE 44.

Baby Gar Safety

Gars lay their eggs on the stems and leaves of water plants. Their eggs are poisonous to the other inhabitants of the estuary, so they are generally left alone. Once the baby fish—called fry—hatch, they have another trick to help them survive. Each gar fry has a special pad on its mouth. This pad sticks the fry to a plant. The fry are much less likely to be eaten when they are attached to plants than when they are swimming freely. Once the gar gets a little bigger, the pad disappears and the gar is on its own in the water.

AN ESTUARY FOOD WEB

In the estuary, energy moves around the food chain from the sun to plants, from plants to plant eaters, and from animals to the creatures that eat them.

NUTRIA
(Myocastor coypus)

As daylight fades along the coast, the nutria wakes in his nest. He looks a little like a beaver or a muskrat, and he is distantly related to both. His nest is a round platform of dead plants he's pulled together. The nutria steps down from his nest and splashes in the shallow water. His front legs are much shorter than his hind ones, so he walks hunched over. But he's still very fast when he needs to be.

The nutria wades through the shallows until he arrives where he left off last night. Then he plunges his front paws in the mud and sand. His sharp claws rip at the roots of the water plants. He pulls them up and bites at them with his large front teeth.

Invasion

Nutria is not a native species to the estuary. It is an invasive species. Nutria came to the United States from South America. There, the nutria is called coypu. They were brought to the Mississippi Delta to be raised and sold for their fur. But when they were released in the wild in the 1930s, they took over. The twenty nutria that were set free grew to twenty million nutria in the wild in just twenty short years. They are a pest and a real threat to the coastline habitat.

You can see where the nutria has been feeding. Tall grasses and water plants edge the water throughout most of the estuary, but where the nutria has eaten, the plants are gone. Even worse, the soil **erodes** as the tides move the water back and forth. Erosion is already a problem in the estuary, and nutria are making it worse.

Last night for dinner, the nutria gobbled...

...**the roots and stems of water plants.** To see what the water plants of the estuary are like, TURN TO PAGE 27.

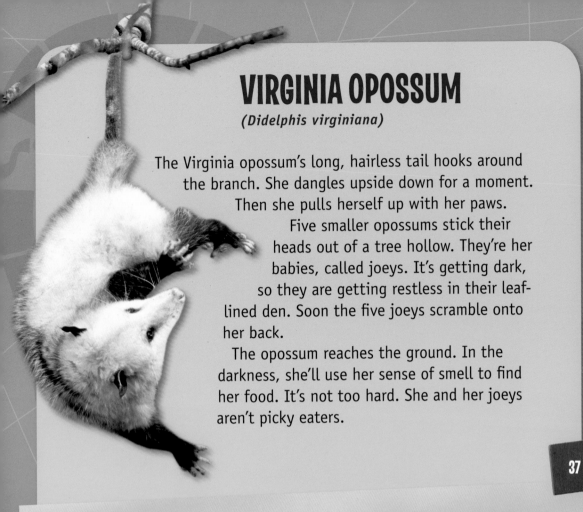

VIRGINIA OPOSSUM
(Didelphis virginiana)

The Virginia opossum's long, hairless tail hooks around the branch. She dangles upside down for a moment. Then she pulls herself up with her paws.

Five smaller opossums stick their heads out of a tree hollow. They're her babies, called joeys. It's getting dark, so they are getting restless in their leaf-lined den. Soon the five joeys scramble onto her back.

The opossum reaches the ground. In the darkness, she'll use her sense of smell to find her food. It's not too hard. She and her joeys aren't picky eaters.

37

This Virginia opossum is playing dead.

The opossum waddles along through the thick brush. Suddenly, she freezes. Something's near. The scent of a fox wafts by, and before she can hide, the fox is there. Immediately, she keels over. So do her joeys.

The fox trots over, eager for a quick meal. The fox sniffs the opossums. Their eyes are open. Their mouths hang open. Their bodies are stiff, and a terrible smell comes from them. He nudges them. To the fox, they seem long dead. The fox isn't a **scavenger**. He likes his meals to be freshly killed. The fox gives up and moves on.

The opossums wait, and then slowly they start moving again. They've fooled the fox.

At the base of a gum tree, the mother opossum scratches in the soft soil. Yum, a juicy grub! She nibbles it. But what's this? Her digging has uncovered even a better meal. Hidden under the dead leaves and branches is a snake! The snake bares its fangs, but the cold night air has made it slow and stiff. The opossum pounces. In moments, she and her babies are munching away on the poisonous snake. Luckily for the opossums, something in their blood keeps the snake **venom** from hurting them.

Last night for dinner, the Virginia opossum nibbled on . . .

. . . a nematode found under a log. To see what another nematode is up to, TURN TO PAGE 16.

. . . a gray bat hanging upside down on a tree branch. To read what another gray bat is up to, TURN TO PAGE 50.

. . . a few flatid planthoppers on the underside of a leaf. To see what other planthoppers are up to, TURN TO PAGE 24.

. . . some biting midges licked off her babies. To see what other biting midges are up to, TURN TO PAGE 56.

Kangaroo Cousin?

Opossums are the only marsupials in North America. That means they carry their young in pouches on their stomachs, as kangaroos and koalas do. When opossum joeys are born, they are about the size of a bean. They crawl into their mother's pouch, where they stay and drink her milk for about two months. When they have grown to the size of a mouse, they crawl out of her pouch. Then they ride on their mother's back. A few weeks later, they head off on their own, all grown up.

TREES OF THE ESTUARY

Many North American forests have hardwood trees—trees with broad leaves that usually change color in the fall. The estuary contains many of the same hardwood trees. Oaks, red maples, alders, and willows tower high in the sky. At the top, trumpet vines lace the treetops together. Lower to the ground, shrubs such as bayberry bushes and poison ivy grow so thickly they make travel difficult. Under them, colorful flowers such as goldenrod and irises bloom.

In the swampier areas of the estuary, hardwood trees can't grow. They need soil where their roots can burrow deep down. In the swamp, the soil contains so much water that roots can't take in air or nutrients. Deep-rooted trees don't survive. Instead, mangroves and cypresses grow in the swamps. Their knobby roots spread wide in a web above the water's surface so that they can take in air. *These trees take in nutrients from . . .*

cypress trees

mangrove trees

. . . a dead nematode floating in the water. To see what another nematode is up to, TURN TO PAGE 16.

. . . a decomposing nutria. To see what another nutria is up to, TURN TO PAGE 35.

. . . a dead northern raccoon. To see what another northern raccoon is up to, TURN TO PAGE 58.

. . . a decomposing ivory-billed woodpecker. To see what another ivory-billed woodpecker is up to, TURN TO PAGE 18.

. . . a drowned bobcat. To see what another bobcat is up to, TURN TO PAGE 19.

COTTONMOUTH *(Agkistrodon piscivorus)*

The young cottonmouth stretches out on the log, soaking up the last rays of sunshine. After spending most of his day swimming in the water, he needs to warm up before the cool night falls. As the sun goes down, the snake slides off the log and curls up in a hollow underneath it.

The darkness deepens. A pig frog hops through the shallows. The frog is barely visible in the dark, but the cottonmouth knows just where it is. A special pit between his eyes tells the cottonmouth what's hot and what's cold around him. The cottonmouth can sense where the frog is because the frog is warmer than the air and ground.

Still, the cottonmouth knows he'll get just one chance to catch the frog. He sticks his tail out into the open. Adult cottonmouths are dark brown, but this one is young. The tip of his tail is bright yellow. The frog hops closer to investigate. When the frog is close enough, the cottonmouth strikes. The snake pumps **venom** into the frog's body. After holding the frog in its mouth for a few minutes, the cottonmouth swallows the frog whole.

Last night for dinner, the cottonmouth swallowed . . .

A cottonmouth swallows a frog.

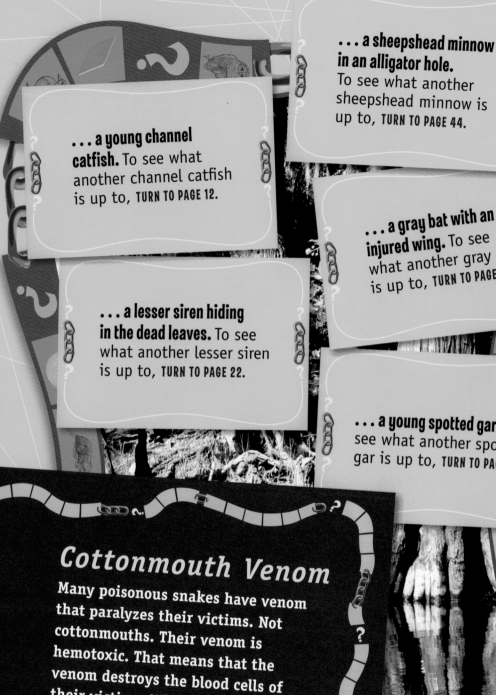

. . . a sheepshead minnow in an alligator hole. To see what another sheepshead minnow is up to, TURN TO PAGE 44.

. . . a young channel catfish. To see what another channel catfish is up to, TURN TO PAGE 12.

. . . a gray bat with an injured wing. To see what another gray bat is up to, TURN TO PAGE 50.

. . . a lesser siren hiding in the dead leaves. To see what another lesser siren is up to, TURN TO PAGE 22.

. . . a young spotted gar. To see what another spotted gar is up to, TURN TO PAGE 32.

Cottonmouth Venom

Many poisonous snakes have venom that paralyzes their victims. Not cottonmouths. Their venom is hemotoxic. That means that the venom destroys the blood cells of their victims. When an animal is bitten by a cottonmouth, the venom makes the blood cells burst inside the victim's body. Eventually, the victim bleeds to death.

SHEEPSHEAD MINNOW *(Cyprinodon variegatus)*

The male sheepshead minnow fans at the sand under the water in the salt marsh. Slowly, the sand shifts, leaving a small indentation. He circles around it. He's usually silver, but now he's bright blue. His blue color tells female sheepshead minnows that he's looking for a mate.

A female swims by. She checks out the hole he made. But she's not impressed. It's not the right nest for her. She keeps swimming. Another female approaches. But she, too, swims on.

Then a male swims by. He's too close. The minnow charges at him. He may be small—only 1.5 inches (4 centimeters)—but he's got teeth. The intruding male scoots out of there fast.

A third female has watched the male defend his nest. She likes what she sees. She swims around in the nest. The male follows her. She decides she'll lay her eggs here. Over the next few weeks, she'll lay almost one thousand eggs in the male's nest. And the male will protect them.

Last night for dinner, the sheepshead minnow ate . . .

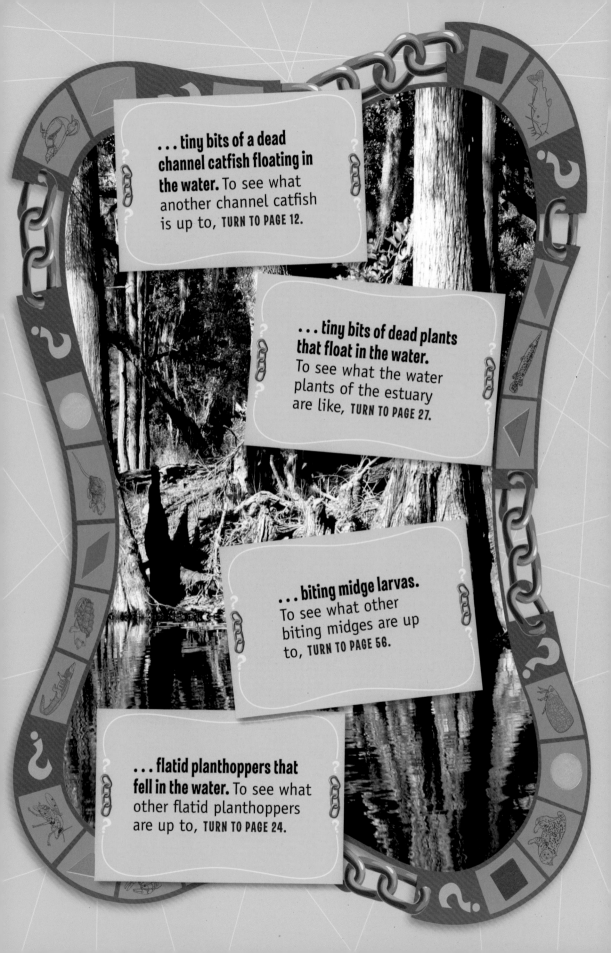

. . . tiny bits of a dead channel catfish floating in the water. To see what another channel catfish is up to, TURN TO PAGE 12.

. . . tiny bits of dead plants that float in the water. To see what the water plants of the estuary are like, TURN TO PAGE 27.

. . . biting midge larvas. To see what other biting midges are up to, TURN TO PAGE 56.

. . . flatid planthoppers that fell in the water. To see what other flatid planthoppers are up to, TURN TO PAGE 24.

WHOOPING CRANE *(Grus americana)*

Uh-oh. This is a **DEAD END**. Whooping cranes are the largest bird in North America, but they are endangered. In 1941, only sixteen of these birds were left. Hunting and habitat destruction had killed the rest. Fortunately that number has grown to more than four hundred in recent years, due to the hard work of concerned humans.

Still, these birds struggle to survive in their natural habitat. Just a few groups remain in the wild, and scientists watch over them carefully. Larger numbers of cranes are being raised in captivity. But these birds often don't learn the instincts needed to survive on their own. Because so many are being raised by people, whooping cranes probably won't become totally extinct. But scientists still don't know if the species will survive in the wild.

ALLIGATOR SNAPPING TURTLE

(Macroclemys temminckii)

Over there, near the beaver dam, a nose pokes up out of the water for a breath. Just for a moment. Then the beaklike snout sinks back under the surface of the water. The alligator snapping turtle only needs to come up for air every forty-five minutes or so. Other than that, he spends nearly his whole life under the water.

Duckweed floats on the water's surface. Underneath, it's dark and murky. Eelgrass and cattails grow up through the duckweed. It's hard to see, and this is how the alligator snapping turtle likes it. He's so still that algae have started to grow on his ridged back. He looks just like a log or a rock or a pile of dead leaves, not like the 175-pound (80-kilogram) predator he is.

He cracks open his mouth. Everything about him is brown and green—except his tongue. Inside his mouth, his pink tongue wiggles and dances. Some fish swimming by stop to investigate. They are curious. It looks just as if a nice worm has fallen into the water.

One fish draws closer. That pink wriggling tongue looks so delicious! The fish can't resist. It darts in for a quick meal.

Snap! The alligator snapping turtle slams his hooked beak closed. The fish is slashed in half by the beak's sharp edges. The alligator snapping turtle gulps down the pieces of the fish. Another meal eaten—and the turtle didn't even have to move!

But that one fish wasn't quite enough. Slowly, the alligator snapping turtle slides through the water. His wide feet push him along. His long tail helps steer him. With his three spiny rows of scales on his back, he looks almost like a plated dinosaur.

He settles in the mud on the other side of the stack of logs and sticks the beavers have cut down. He sucks water in and out of his throat. Doing this helps him to sense chemicals that potential **prey** give off. He senses something in the soft mud. He scrapes, and a smaller turtle scoots out of the mud. Snap! The alligator snapping turtle eats him too.

Last night for dinner, the alligator snapping turtle swallowed . . .

A female alligator snapping turtle with her young

Brothers or Sisters?

One of the only times alligator snapping turtles leave the water is when females lay eggs. They lay their eggs in a shallow hole on the shore near water. Scientists have found that the air temperature determines whether the turtle eggs are males or females. If the weather is cold, the eggs will be almost all female. If the weather is warm, the eggs will hatch male turtles. And if somewhere in between? Then the eggs will be a mix of females and males.

. . . **an American alligator hatchling.** To see what an American alligator is up to, TURN TO PAGE 8.

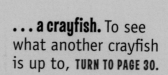

. . . **a crayfish.** To see what another crayfish is up to, TURN TO PAGE 30.

. . . **a channel catfish that couldn't resist the turtle tongue.** To see what another channel catfish is up to, TURN TO PAGE 12.

. . . **a young spotted gar.** To see what another spotted gar is up to, TURN TO PAGE 32.

. . . **a wood duckling that wandered too far from its mother.** To see what other wood ducklings are up to, TURN TO PAGE 14.

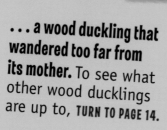

. . . **several sheepshead minnows.** To see what other sheepshead minnows are up to, TURN TO PAGE 44.

. . . **a lesser siren.** To see what another lesser siren is up to, TURN TO PAGE 22.

GRAY BAT *(Myotis grisescens)*

Gray bats used to flap through the night skies of the Mississippi Delta estuary. They'd skim the water's surface and gobble up flying insects and water bugs. But these days, medium-sized bats are rarely seen. They live in huge groups in caves, but as more people explore and visit caves, these bats are disturbed. When they are interrupted at their roosting site, the mother bats get flustered and drop their babies. If they are bothered repeatedly, the entire bat colony will abandon the cave. Since these bats only live in a few caves worldwide, every time this happens, it is disastrous. This is a *DEAD END*.

SWAMP RABBIT *(Sylvilagus aquaticus)*

The swamp rabbit huddles in his nest in the tall grass. At 20 inches (51 centimeters) long, he's the biggest of the cottontail rabbits. His size doesn't protect him from predators, such as the coyote sniffing around nearby.

Suddenly, the coyote sticks his nose through the grass. The rabbit springs into action. His powerful hind legs push him forward into a run. He can run at speeds up to 45 miles (72 kilometers) per hour. Still, the coyote is close on his tail. The rabbit zigs and zags, avoiding the coyote.

The rabbit dashes for a hollow log. But a loud thumping comes from the other end. This log is occupied by another rabbit. He's thumping his hind legs to show he's not willing to share. The first rabbit streaks to the water's edge. The coyote is right behind him. Without hesitating, the rabbit jumps into the water. Splash! He swims out to a clump of tall weeds. He hides, panting, only his nose sticking out of the water.

The coyote wades in after the rabbit. But the rabbit's scent is gone in the water. The coyote gives up. He trots back to shore in search of easier prey. Maybe that other rabbit is still in that hollow log.

Last night for dinner, the swamp rabbit nibbled on . . .

. . . the roots, stems, and leaves of water plants. To see what the water plants of the estuary are like, TURN TO PAGE 27.

. . . the roots, stems, and leaves of the estuary's trees. To see what the trees of the estuary are like, TURN TO PAGE 40.

BARRED OWL
(Strix varia)

Night falls, and the barred owl sticks his face out of a hole in a tree. He stretches out his wings and glides to another tree. He perches on a branch. His large eyes scan the ground below. The light-colored feathers on his face circle his eyes. They help reflect light so he can see even better in the dark.

A mouse scurries through the brush below. The owl takes off. His fringed and fluffy flying feathers make his flight through the estuary skies almost silent. The mouse doesn't stand a chance.

The owl pounces, scooping up the mouse in his sharp talons. A powerful pump of his 24-inch (61-centimeter) wings, and he flaps back up. He carries the mouse, still squirming a bit in his talon, to the hole in the first tree. There his mate pokes her head out. She gulps down the mouse. She's been sitting on their eggs, and she depends on the male owl for food. They've been a team for a long time and will stay together for the rest of their lives.

Once his mate is fed, the male owl swoops back to his hunting perch. He's got the rest of the night to catch his meal.

Last night for dinner, the barred owl caught . . .

A Barred Owl Near You?

Barred owls live in a lot of places, not just in the Mississippi Delta estuary. They are found in many woods and forests across North America. Barred owls like to call at night. So if you find yourself in the woods at night, listen for their calls. Some say it sounds like, "Who cooks for you? Who cooks for you-all?" And if you call them,

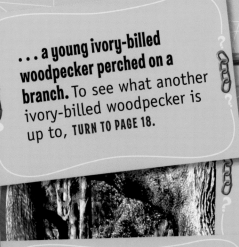

. . . **a young ivory-billed woodpecker perched on a branch.** To see what another ivory-billed woodpecker is up to, TURN TO PAGE 18.

. . . **a cottonmouth slithering through the leaves.** To see what another cottonmouth is up to, TURN TO PAGE 42.

. . . **a bobcat kitten whose mother was killed.** To see what another bobcat is up to, TURN TO PAGE 19.

. . . **a sheepshead minnow.** To see what other sheepshead minnows are up to, TURN TO PAGE 44.

. . . **a nutria grazing on some leaves.** To see what another nutria is up to, TURN TO PAGE 35.

. . . **a gray bat roosting on a branch.** To see what another gray bat is up to, TURN TO PAGE 50.

. . . **a swamp rabbit hopping through the forest.** To see what another swamp rabbit is up to, TURN TO PAGE 51.

. . . **a Virginia opossum crawling on a log.** To see what another Virginia opossum is up to, TURN TO PAGE 37.

BITING MIDGE (Ceratopogonidae family)

See that cloud of biting midges over there? No? Well, that's no surprise. Biting midges are sometimes called "no-see-ums" because they are so tiny and hard to see. Don't worry if you can't see them. You'll know they're around soon enough. The bites from a female sting, much like a mosquito bite does.

That female over there is laying eggs in the sand—450 of them at a time. When the eggs hatch, the midge **larvas** will eat the tiny bits of dead plants and animals in the sand. That makes them decomposers. Decomposers are an important part of the food web because they get rid of decaying material.

Soon, the larva will grow bigger and become a **pupa**. When it hatches, it is a fly. The flies buzz off on their first flights from the sand. And that's why biting midges sometimes are called sand flies.

Last night for dinner, the male biting midges dined on ...

56

... **juices from trees and moss.** To see what the trees of the estuary are like, TURN TO PAGE 40.

... **juices from water plants.** To see what the water plants of the estuary are like, TURN TO PAGE 27.

midges swarming

Last night for dinner, the female biting midges dined on . . .

. . . **the blood from a bobcat.** To see what another bobcat is up to, TURN TO PAGE 19.

. . . **the blood from a barred owl.** To see what another barred owl is up to, TURN TO PAGE 53.

NORTHERN RACCOON *(Procyon lotor)*

The young northern raccoon fluffs the dry leaves in the hole in the tree. He just left his mother and siblings last spring. This year he is in his own den and must find his own food. So far, it's been hard work. It's dark, so it's time to eat. He shuffles out onto a tree branch. Whoops! His hind legs slip, and he crashes down to the bushes below. He shakes himself. The 20-foot (6-meter) fall doesn't slow him at all.

The raccoon makes his way to the water's edge. Maybe he'll be lucky and find some clams or mussels. Some nights, he returns home without eating anything.

He digs in the sand. Yes, here's a clam! With his delicate five-fingered paws, he pries the shell open. Then he sticks his snout in and slurps down the insides. The raccoon is lucky to find such a meal. Although raccoons will eat just about anything, they have a hard time finding food. Most raccoons don't live past their second year.

Last night for dinner, the northern raccoon gobbled down...

58

. . . **a crayfish fished out of the water.** To see what another crayfish is up to, TURN TO PAGE 30.

. . . **American alligator eggs that didn't hatch.** To see what an American alligator is up to, TURN TO PAGE 8.

. . . **whooping crane eggs hidden in the grass.** To see what a whooping crane is up to, TURN TO PAGE 46.

. . . **a wood duck egg.** To see what a wood duck is up to, TURN TO PAGE 14.

. . . **alligator snapping turtle eggs dug out of the sand.** To see what an alligator snapping turtle is up to, TURN TO PAGE 47.

. . . **ivory-billed woodpecker eggs.** To see what an ivory-billed woodpecker is up to, TURN TO PAGE 18.

. . . **a barred owl egg.** To see what a barred owl is up to, TURN TO PAGE 53.

. . . **anhinga eggs left unattended.** To see what an anhinga is up to, TURN TO PAGE 25.

GLOSSARY

amphibians: animals that live both on land and in water

bacteria: tiny living things made up of only one cell

brackish: slightly salty

carnivore: an animal that eats other animals

decomposers: living things, such as insects or bacteria, that feed on dead plants and animals

endangered: a type of living thing that is in danger of dying out

erode: to wear away

extinct: no longer existing

food chain: a system in which energy moves from the sun to plants and to animals as each eats and is eaten

food web: many food chains linked together

habitat: the place where an animal lives

larvas: the wormlike stage in an insect's life between the egg and adult forms

native: a plant or animal that grows naturally in a certain habitat

nutrients: substances, especially in food, that help a plant or animal survive

parasites: living things that live in or on other living things that they usually harm

predators: animals that hunt and kill other animals for food

prey: an animal that is hunted for food by another animal

primary consumers: animals that eat plants

producer: a living thing, such as a plant, that makes its own food from nonliving things, such as sunlight and air

pupa: a stage in an insect's life between larva and adult

scavengers: an animal that eats dead plants or animals

secondary consumers: animals and insects that eat other animals and insects

species: a group of related animals or plants

tertiary consumers: animals that eat other animals and have few natural enemies

venom: poison

FURTHER READING AND WEBSITES

Animals
http://animals.nationalgeographic.com/
Find your favorite estuary animal in this comprehensive guide to animals around the world.

Arnosky, Jim. *Babies in the Bayou*. New York: G. P. Putnam's Sons, 2007. This gentle picture book follows animals and their young through a swamp.

Blaustein, Daniel. *The Everglades and the Gulf Coast*. New York: Benchmark Books, 2000. Learn more about these two endangered habitats and the animals that live in them.

Exploring Estuaries
http://www.epa.gov/owow/estuaries/kids/
Learn more about estuaries in general, and then take a virtual visit to the Barataria Terrebonne estuarine complex.

Fleisher, Paul. *Salt Marsh*. New York: Benchmark Books, 1999. Find out more about the salt marshes in the estuary.

Johansson, Philip. *Marshes and Swamps: A Wetland Web of Life*. Berkeley Heights, NJ: Enslow Publishers, 2008. Food webs in different types of marshes and swamps are featured.

Kids' Page
http://www.aquariumteacher.com/kids.html
Read a quick overview of what an estuary is and why we need estuaries.

Lion, David C. *A Home in the Swamp*. New York: Children's Press, 2006. What's life like in a swamp? Find out who lives there and how they survive.

Mudd-Ruth, Maria. *The Mississippi River*. New York: Benchmark Books, 2001. This book covers the plants and animals along the whole length of the Mississippi River. Learn about where the river water has been before it comes to the Gulf.

Rockwell, Anne F. *Who Lives in an Alligator Hole?* New York: Collins, 2006. Alligators create their own habitats when they dig out a hole to live in. See what animals come to live with the alligators.

Walker, Sally M. *Life in an Estuary*. Minneapolis: Twenty-First Century Books, 2003. Take a look at another North American estuary—the Chesapeake Bay on the U.S. East Coast—in this book. Learn how the Chesapeake formed thousands of years ago. And learn about all the unusual plants and animals that make their homes in this ecosystem.

Yolen, Jane. *Welcome to the River of Grass*. New York: Putnam's, 2001. The river of grass refers to the Everglades, but the Everglades share many of the same plants and animals as the Mississippi estuary.

SELECTED BIBLIOGRAPHY

Barataria Terrebonne National Estuary Program. *BTNEP*. January 2008. http://www.btnep.org/home.asp (February 14, 2009).

Behler, John L. *National Audubon Society Field Guide to North American Reptiles and Amphibians*. New York: Knopf, 1979.

Bull, John, and John Farrand Jr. *The National Audubon Society Field Guide to North American Birds Eastern Region*. New York: Knopf, 1994.

Burnie, David, and Don E. Wilson. *Animal: The Definitive Visual Guide to the World's Wildlife*. London: DK, 2005.

EPA. "National Estuaries Program." *Environmental Protection Agency*. June 2009. http://www.epa.gov/owow/estuaries/ (February 14, 2009).

McKay, George, ed. *The Encyclopedia of Animals: A Complete Visual Guide*. Berkeley: University of California Press, 2004.

Milne, Lorus Johnson. *National Audubon Society Field Guide to North American Insects and Spiders*. New York: A. A. Knopf, 1980.

National Park Service. "Jean Lafitte Natural Historical Park and Preserve." *nps. gov.* May 2009.
http://www.nps.gov/jela/ (February 14, 2009).

Tidwell, Mike. *Bayou Farewell: The Rich Life and Tragic Death of Louisiana's Cajun Coast*. New York: Pantheon Books, 2003.

University of Michigan. *Museum of Zoology's Animal Diversity Web*. 2008. http://animaldiversity.ummz.umich.edu/site/index.html (February 15, 2009).

WWF. *Wildfinder*. 2008. http://www.worldwildlife.org/wildfinder/ (February 14, 2009).

INDEX

Photo Acknowledgments

The images in this book are used with the permission of: © Sumos/Dreamstime.com, pp. 1, 4-5, 6-7, 11, 13, 15, 17, 21, 23, 26, 29, 31, 33, 39, 41, 43, 45, 49, 55, 59; © Adpower99/Dreamstime.com, p. 8 (top); © iStockphoto.com/Todd Winner, p. 8 (bottom); © Henry, P./Peter Arnold, Inc., p. 9; © Thomas & Pat Leeson/Photo Researchers, Inc., p. 10; U.S. Fish and Wildlife Service, pp. 12, 14 (top), 30, 32, 40 (top); © Steve Maslowski/Visuals Unlimited/Getty Images, pp. 14 (bottom), 37 (top); © Nigel Cattlin/Alamy, p. 16 (top); © The Natural History Museum/Alamy, p. 16 (bottom); © John Cancalosi/Peter Arnold, Inc., p. 18; © Lee Cates/Photodisc/Getty Images, p. 19; © age fotostock/SuperStock, pp. 20, 54; © Biosphoto/Daniel Heuclin/Peter Arnold, Inc., p. 22; © M. & C. Photography/Peter Arnold, Inc., p. 24; © Jeff Foott/Discovery Channel Images/Getty Images, p. 25 (top); © Karlene Schwartz, pp. 25 (bottom), 27 (top), 28 (middle), 40 (bottom); © Mark Conlin/Alamy, p. 28 (top); © Marc Epstein/Visuals Unlimited, Inc., p. 28 (bottom); © Inga Spence/Visuals Unlimited/Getty Images, p. 35; © iStockphoto.com/Gary Ward, p. 36; © Frank Lukasseck/Photographer's Choice/Getty Images, p. 37 (bottom); © William Grenfell/Visuals Unlimited, Inc., p. 38; © Daniel Heuclin/NHPA/Photoshot, p. 42 (top); © Paulwolf/Dreamstime.com, p. 42 (bottom); © Fred Whitehead/Animals Animals, p. 44; © Jewhyte/Dreamstime.com, p. 46; © Karl H. Switak/Photo Researchers, Inc., p. 47; © Millard H. Sharp/Photo Researchers, Inc., p. 48; © Jeff Lepore/Photo Researchers, Inc., p. 50; © David Welling/naturepl.com, p. 51; © George D. Lepp/CORBIS, p. 52; © James Urbach/SuperStock, p. 53; © Jscalev/Dreamstime.com, p. 56; © Mark Bowler/Alamy, p. 57; © Carl R. Sams II/Peter Arnold, Inc., p. 58. Illustrations and map: © Laura Westlund and Bill Hauser/Independent Picture Service.

Front Cover: © Sumos/Dreamstime.com (background); © iStockphoto.com/clark42 (left); © Steve Maslowski/Visuals Unlimited/Getty Images (second from left); © Ragnar Schmuck/fStop/Getty Images (second from right); © Riccardo Savi/The Image Bank/Getty Images (right).

About the Authors

Don and Becky Wojahn are school library media specialists by day and writers by night. Their natural habitat is the temperate forests of northwestern Wisconsin, where they share their den with two animal-loving sons and two big black dogs. The Wojahns are the authors of all twelve books in the Follow That Food Chain series.